Based on the best-selling keyboard method *by Kenneth Baker*.

THE COMPLETE KEYBOARD PLAYER

Number Ones

Wise Publications
part of The Music Sales Group
London/New York/Paris/Sydney/Copenhagen/Berlin/Madrid/Tokyo

Master Chord Chart

C

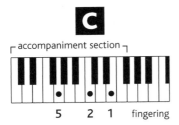

5   2   1   fingering

Cm

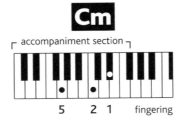

5   2   1   fingering

C7

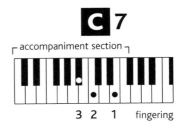

3   2   1   fingering

D♭(C#)

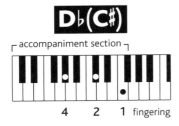

4   2   1   fingering

D♭(C#)m

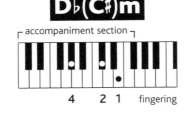

4   2   1   fingering

D♭(C#)7

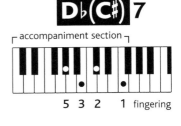

5   3   2   1   fingering

D

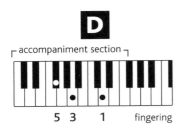

5   3   1   fingering

Dm

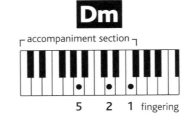

5   2   1   fingering

D7

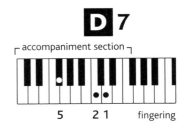

5   2 1   fingering

E♭(D#)

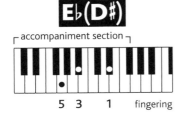

5   3   1   fingering

E♭(D#)m

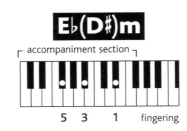

5   3   1   fingering

E♭(D#)7

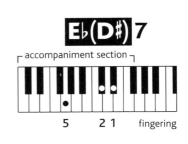

5   2 1   fingering

E

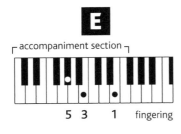

5   3   1   fingering

Em

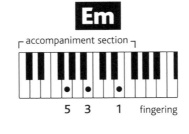

5   3   1   fingering

E7

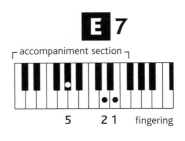

5   2 1   fingering

F

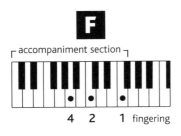

4   2   1   fingering

Fm

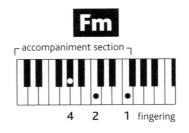

4   2   1   fingering

F7

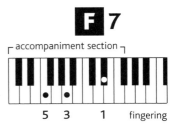

5   3   1   fingering

Master Chord Chart

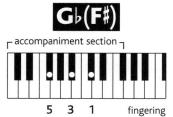

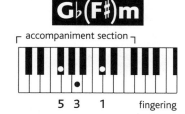

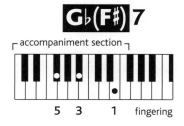

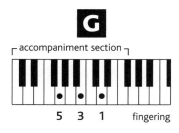

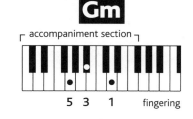

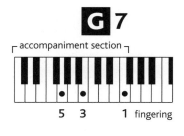

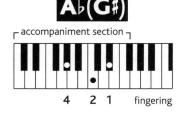

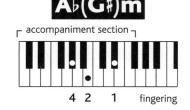

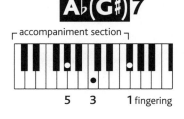

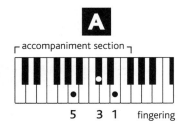

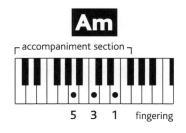

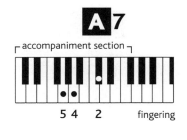

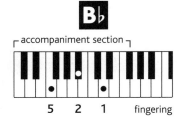

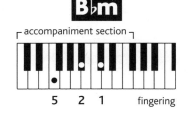

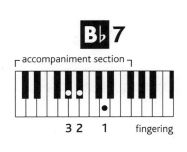

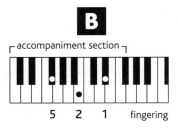

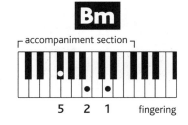

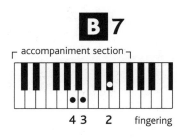

3

All You Need Is Love

Words & Music by John Lennon & Paul McCartney

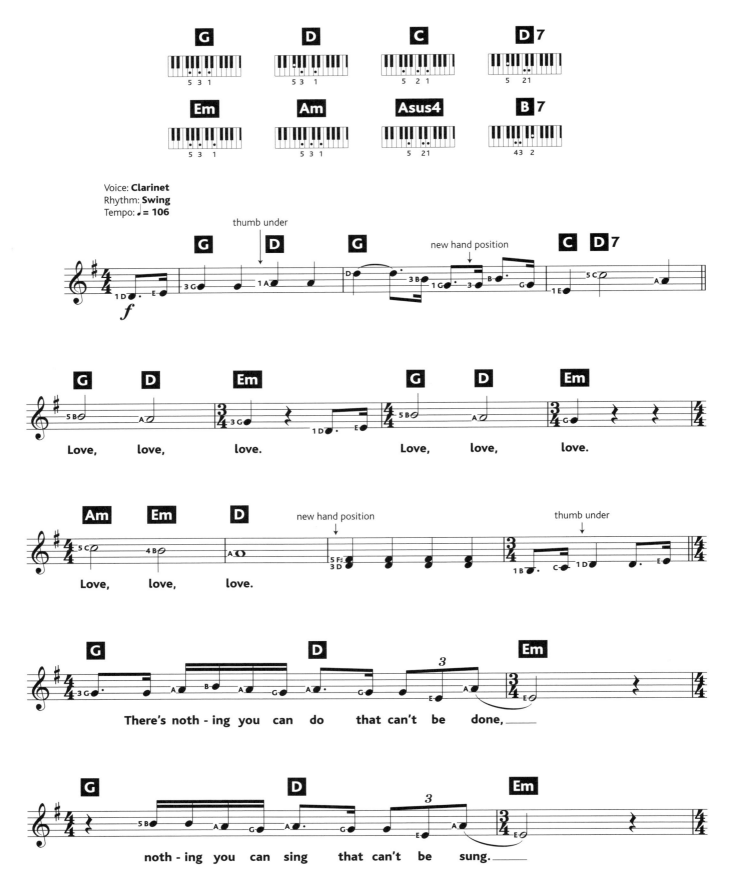

Noth - ing you can say but you can learn how to play the game, — it's

eas - y. There's noth - ing you can make that can't be made, —

— no-one you can save that can't be saved. —

Noth - ing you can do but you can learn how to be you in time it's

eas - y.

All you need is love. —

All you need is love. — All you need is love, —

Em · · · · · · · · · C · · · · · D 7
love. Love is all you need.

G · · · D · · · Em · · · G · · · D
Love, love, love. Love, love,

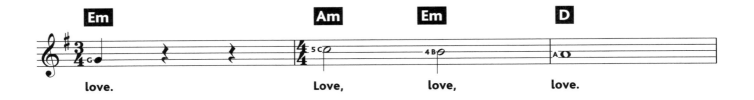

Em · · · · · Am · · · Em · · · D
love. Love, love, love.

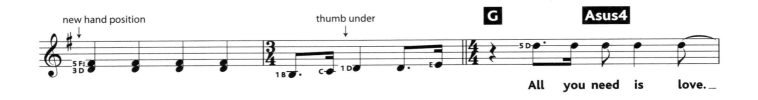

new hand position · · · thumb under · · · G · · · Asus4
All you need is love.

D · · · 2nd finger over · · · G · · · Asus4
All you need is love.

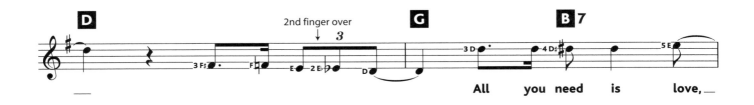

D · · · 2nd finger over · · · G · · · B 7
All you need is love,

Em · · · · · C · · · D 7 · · · G
love. Love is all you need. stop rhythm here

Don't Go Breaking My Heart

Words & Music by Ann Orson & Carte Blanche

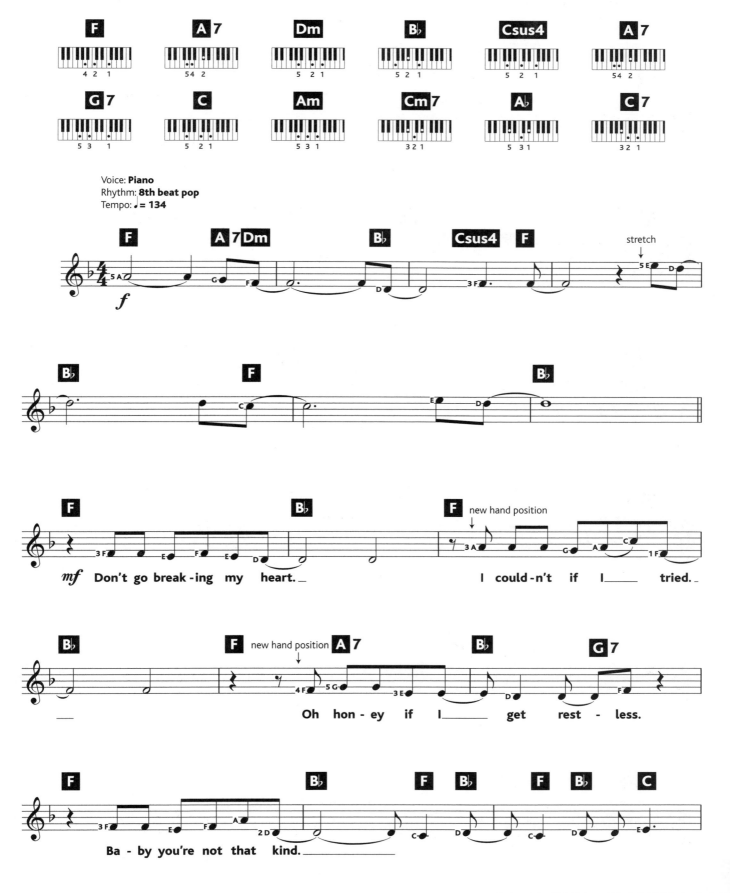

Don't go break-ing my heart. ___ You take the weight off of me. ___

___ Oh hon - ey when you knock on my door. ___

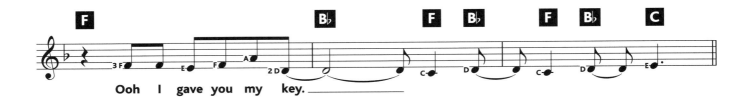

Ooh I gave you my key. _____

f Ooh, ooh, and no-bod-y knows ___ it.

When I was down, ___ I was your clown. ___ Ooh, ooh,

no-bod-y knows ___ it, no-bod-y knows ___ it.

Right from the start, ___ I gave you my heart. ___ Oh, ___

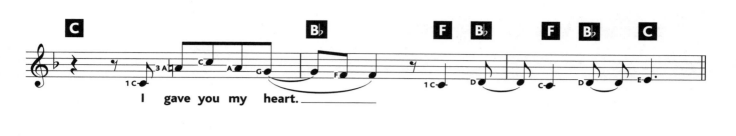

I gave you my heart. _____

Don't go break-ing my heart. _____ I won't go break-ing your heart. _

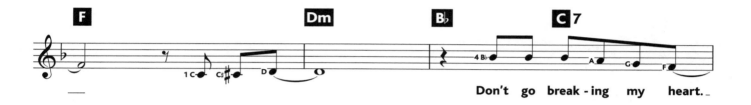

_____ Don't go break-ing my heart. _

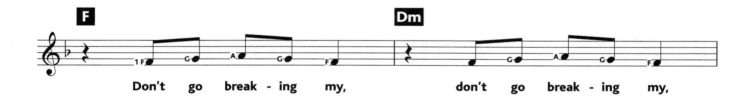

Don't go break-ing my, don't go break-ing my,

I won't go break-ing your heart. ___ Don't go break-ing my,

don't go break-ing my, I won't go break-ing your heart. ___

stop rhythm here

9

Beautiful Day

Words by Bono
Music by U2

Voice: **Acoustic guitar**
Rhythm: **Bright rock**
Tempo: ♩ = 136

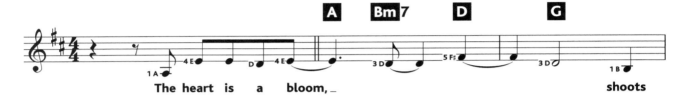

The heart is a bloom, ___ shoots

up through the sto - ny ground. ___ But there's no room, ___

no space to rent in this town. ___ You're out of luck, ___

___ and the rea - son that you had to care. ___

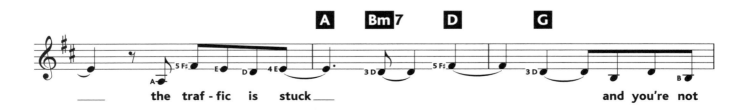

___ the traf - fic is stuck ___ and you're not

mov - in' an - y - where. You though you'd found ___ a friend ___

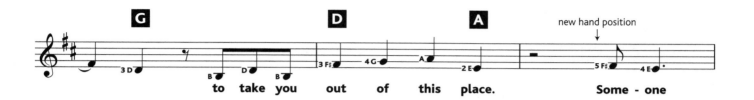

to take you out of this place. Some - one

you could ___ lend a hand in re - turn for grace. ___ S'a beau - ti - ful day. ___

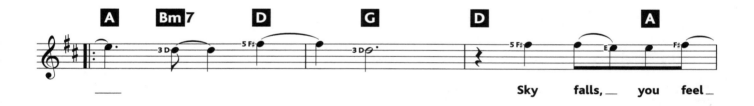

Sky falls, ___ you feel ___

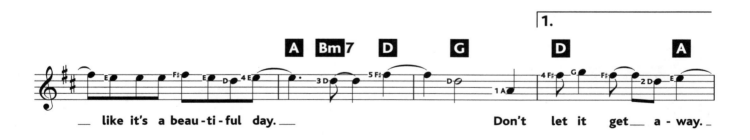

1.

___ like it's a beau - ti - ful day. ___ Don't let it get ___ a - way. ___

2.

___ S'a beau - ti - ful day. ___ let it get ___ a - way. ___

11

Like A Prayer

Words & Music by Madonna & Pat Leonard

Voice: **Saxophone**
Rhythm: **Pop**
Tempo: ♩ = 114

Life is a mys - ter - y,___ ev -'ry - one must stand a - lone.___

___ I hear you call my name___ and it feels like home.___

When you call my name___ it's like a lit - tle___ prayer.___

___ I'm down on my___ knees,___ I wan - na take you

there. In the mid - night hour___ I can feel___ you pow -

-er just like a_____ prayer.___ You know I'll take you

there. I hear your voice,___ it's like an an -

- gel sigh - ing. I have no choice,___ I hear your

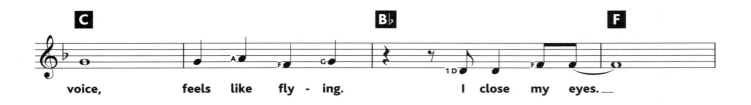

voice, feels like fly - ing. I close my eyes.___

Oh God, I think I'm fall - ing out of the

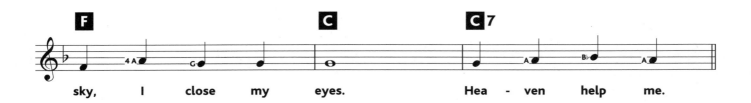

sky, I close my eyes. Hea - ven help me.

When you call my name it's like a lit-tle prayer. I'm down on my knees,

I wan-na take you there. In the mid-night hour I can feel you pow-

-er just like a prayer. You know I'll take you there. When you call my name

it's like a lit-tle prayer. I'm down on my knees, I wan-na take you

there. In the mid-night hour I can feel your pow-

-er just like a prayer. You know I'll take you there.

stop rhythm here

14

Nothing Compares 2 U

Words & Music by Prince

Voice: **Electric piano**
Rhythm: **8th beat**
Tempo: ♩ = 62

1. It's been se-ven hours_ and_ fif-teen days_

new hand position

new hand position

since U took your love a-way. _

I go out ev-'ry night_ and_ sleep all day_____

new hand position

since U took your love a-way. _

Since U been gone I can do what-ev-er I want. _____

I can see whom - ev - er I choose.

I can eat my din - ner in a fan - cy res - tau - rant but

no - thing, I said, no - thing can take a - way these blues. 'Cos no - thing com - pares,

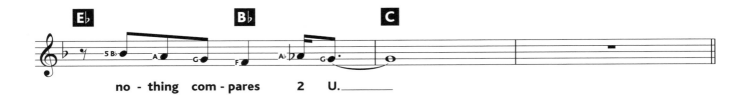

no - thing com - pares 2 U.

2. It's been so lone - ly with - out U here.

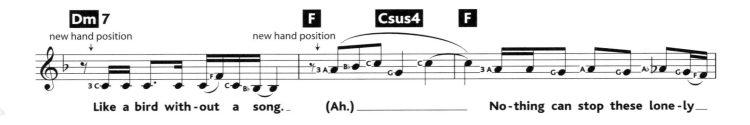

Like a bird with - out a song. (Ah.) No - thing can stop these lone - ly

tears from fall - ing. Tell me, ba - by, where did I go

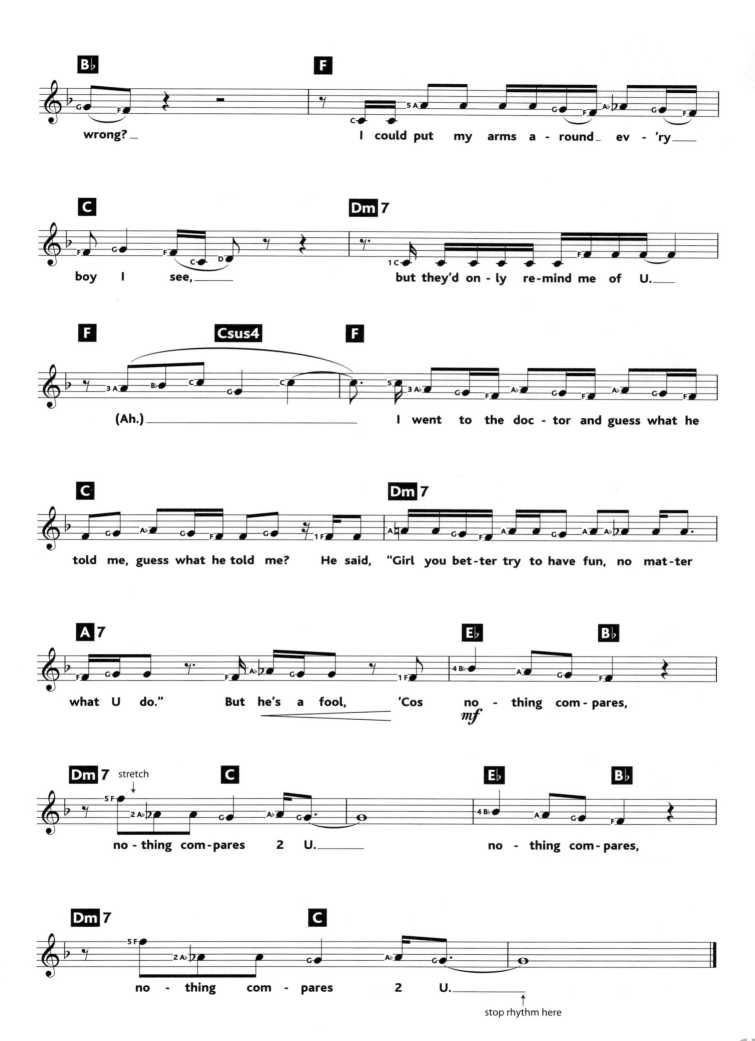

One Night

Words & Music by Dave Bartholomew, Pearl King & Anita Steiman

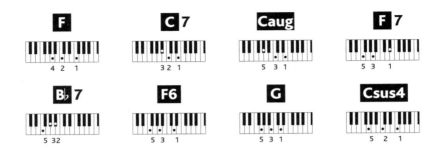

Voice: **Electric guitar**
Rhythm: **Rock 'n' roll**
Tempo: ♩ = 80

One night with you is what I'm now pray-ing for.

start rhythm here

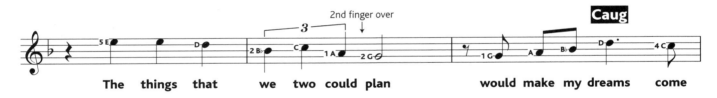

The things that we two could plan would make my dreams come

true. Just call my name, and I'll be

right by your side. I want your sweet help-ing hand,

my love's too strong to hide.

Al-ways lived   a   ver - y qui - et life,   I ain't nev - er did no

wrong.   Now   I   know   that   life   with - out   you____   has

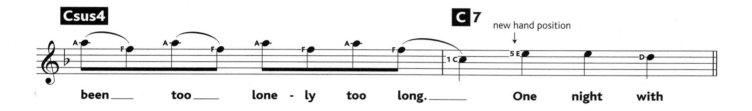

been____   too____   lone - ly   too   long.____   One   night   with

you   is   what   I'm   now   pray - ing   for.

The   things   that   we   two could plan   would make my dreams   come

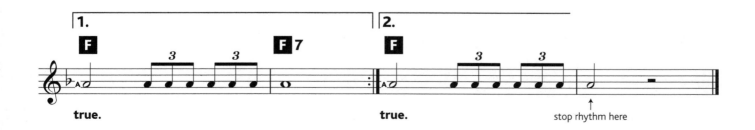

true.   true.

Red, Red Wine

Words & Music by Neil Diamond

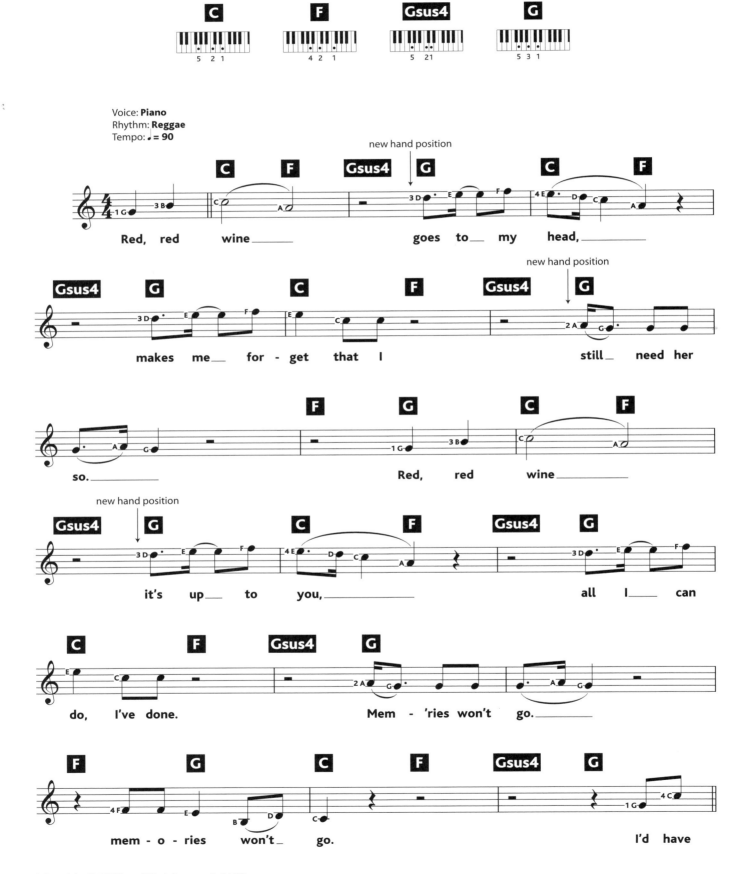

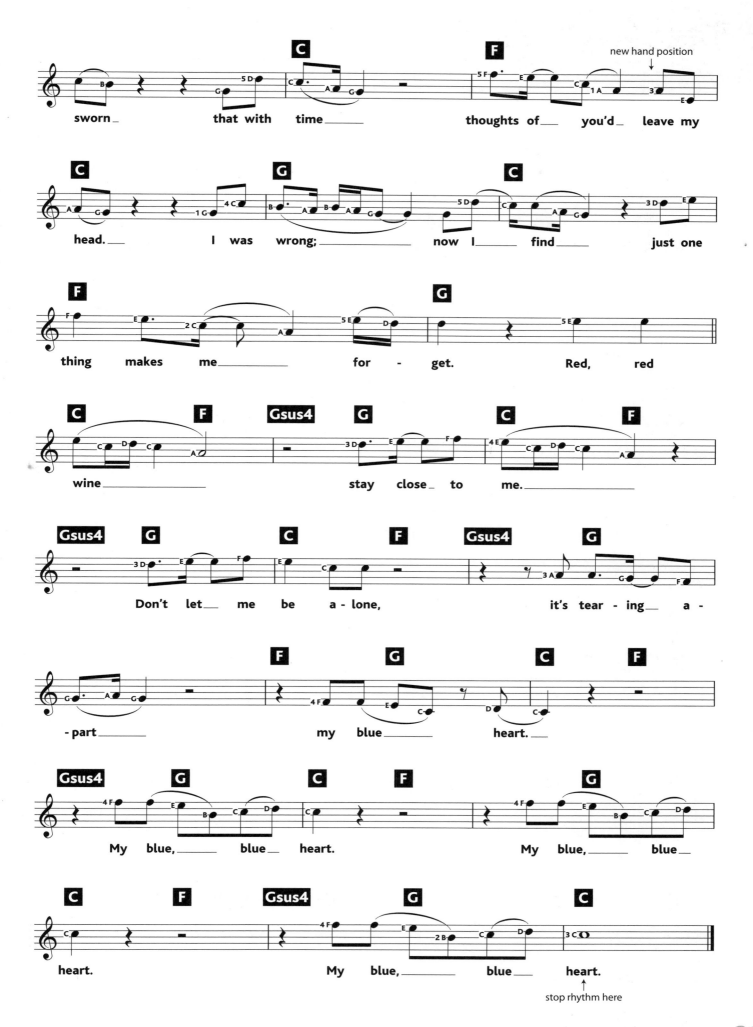

Shine

Words & Music by Mark Owen, Gary Barlow, Stephen Robson, Jason Orange & Howard Donald

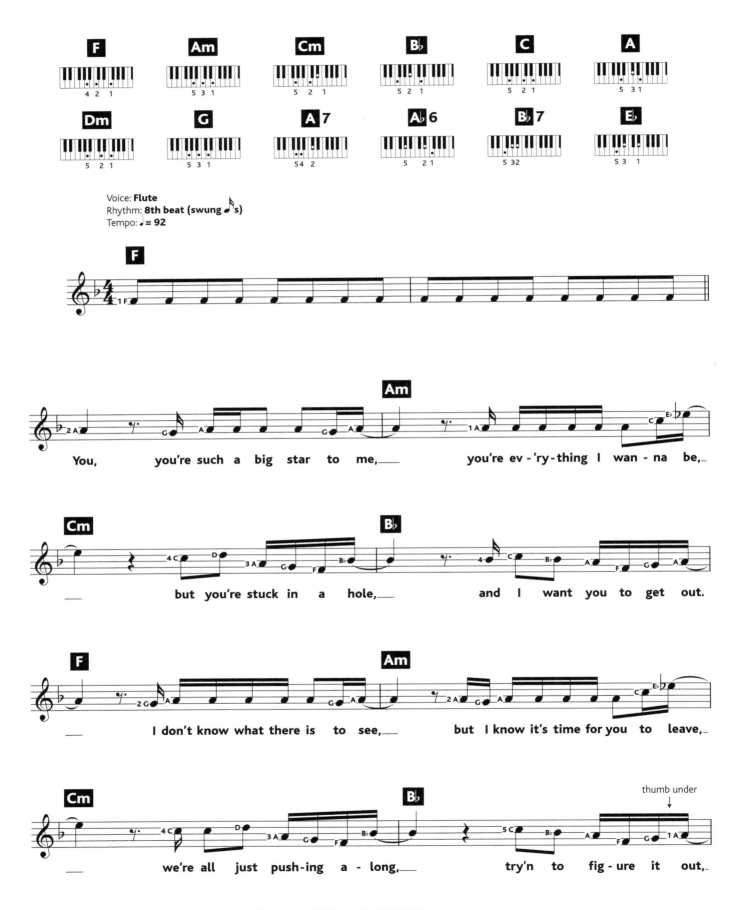

out, out. All your an - tic - i - pa - tion pulls you

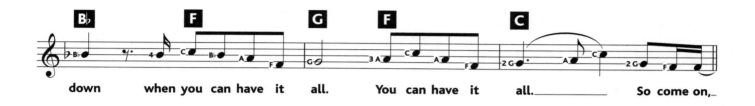

down when you can have it all. You can have it all._____ So come on,__

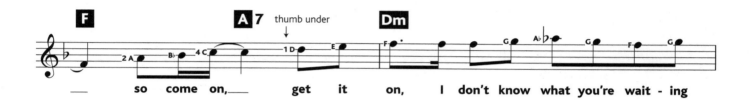

__ so come on,___ get it on, I don't know what you're wait - ing

for, your time is com - ing, don't be late.__ Hey, hey.__ So come on__

__ see the light__ on your face let it shine, just let it

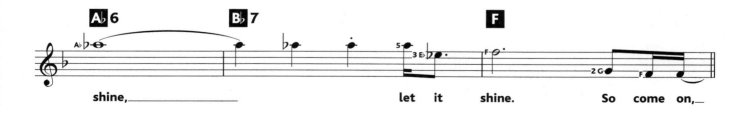

shine,_____ let it shine. So come on,__

so come on, ___ get it on, I don't know what you're wait - ing

for, your time is com - ing, don't be late. ___ Hey, hey. ___ So come on ___

___ see the light ___ on your face let it shine, just let it

shine, _____ let it shine. Oh, come on ___

___ see the light ___ on your face let it shine, just let it

shine, _____ shine. _____

stop rhythm here

Show Me Heaven

Words & Music by Maria McKee, Jay Rifkin & Eric Rackin

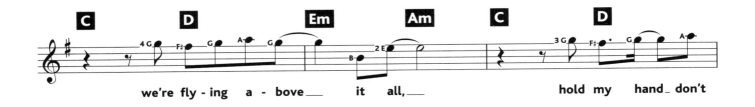

we're fly - ing a - bove___ it all,___ hold my hand_ don't

let me fall.____ You've such a - maz - ing

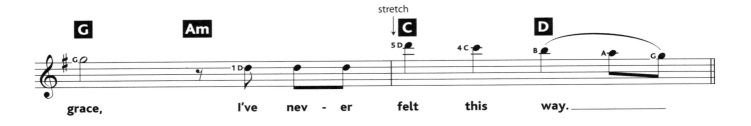

grace, I've nev - er felt this way._____

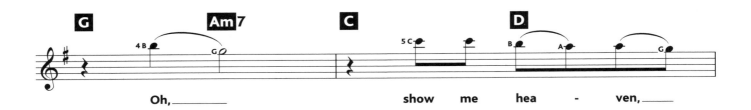

Oh,_____ show me hea - ven,_____

co - ver_ me,___ leave me breath - less.___ Oh,_____

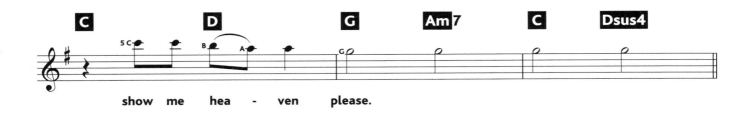

show me hea - ven please.

26

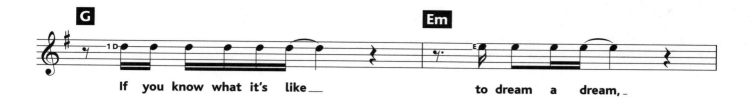

If you know what it's like   to dream a dream,

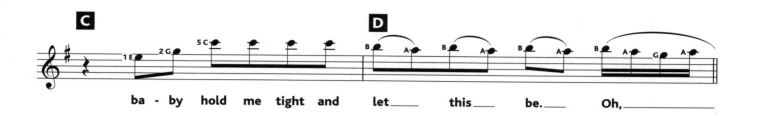

ba - by hold me tight and let   this   be.   Oh,

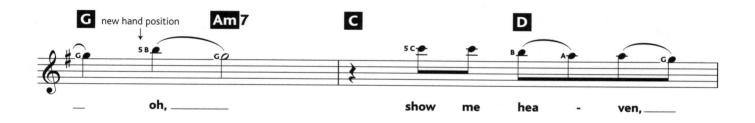

new hand position

— oh,   show me hea - ven,

co - ver me, leave me breath - less. Oh,

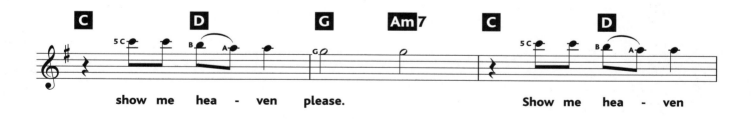

show me hea - ven please.   Show me hea - ven

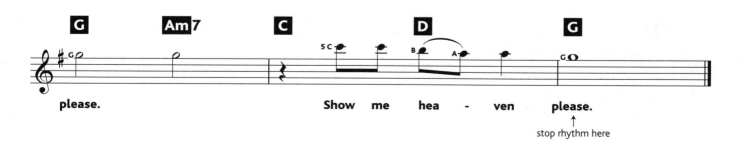

please.   Show me hea - ven please.

stop rhythm here

27

Somethin' Stupid

Words & Music by C. Carson Parks

stretch
G   thumb under   G7

af - ter - wards we drop in - to a qui - et lit - tle place and have a
time is right, your per - fume fills my head, the stars get red and oh, the

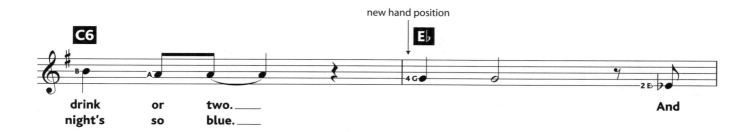

C6   new hand position   E♭

drink or two. _____ And
night's so blue. _____

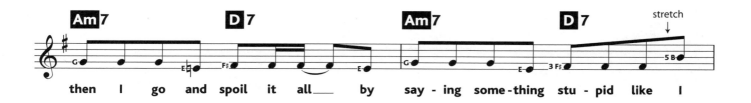

Am7   D7   Am7   D7   stretch

then I go and spoil it all_____ by say - ing some - thing stu - pid like I

1.
G   thumb under

love_____ you. _____ I can see it in your eyes you still de -

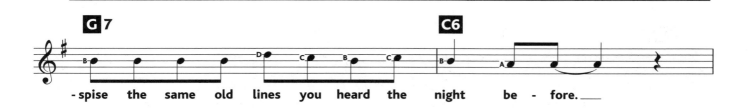

G7   C6

- spise the same old lines you heard the night be - fore. _____

A

And though it's just a line to you, for

29

me   it's   true   and   nev - er   seemed   so   right   be - fore. ___

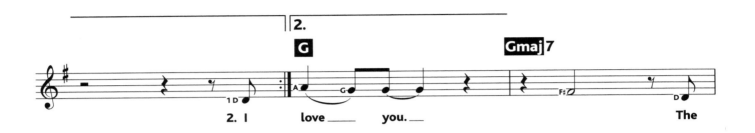

2. I   love ___ you. ___   The

time   is   right,   your   per - fume   fills   my   head,   the   stars   get   red   and   oh,   the

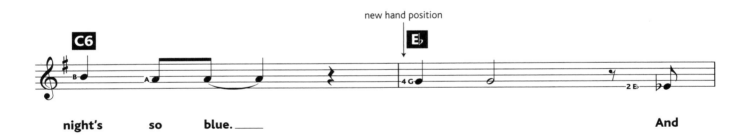

night's   so   blue. ___   And

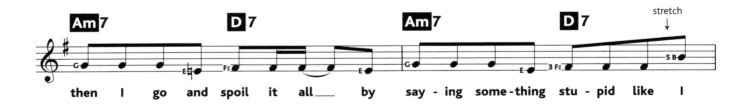

then   I   go   and   spoil   it   all ___   by   say - ing   some - thing   stu - pid   like   I

love ___   you. ___

There Must Be An Angel (Playing With My Heart)

Words & Music by Annie Lennox & David A. Stewart

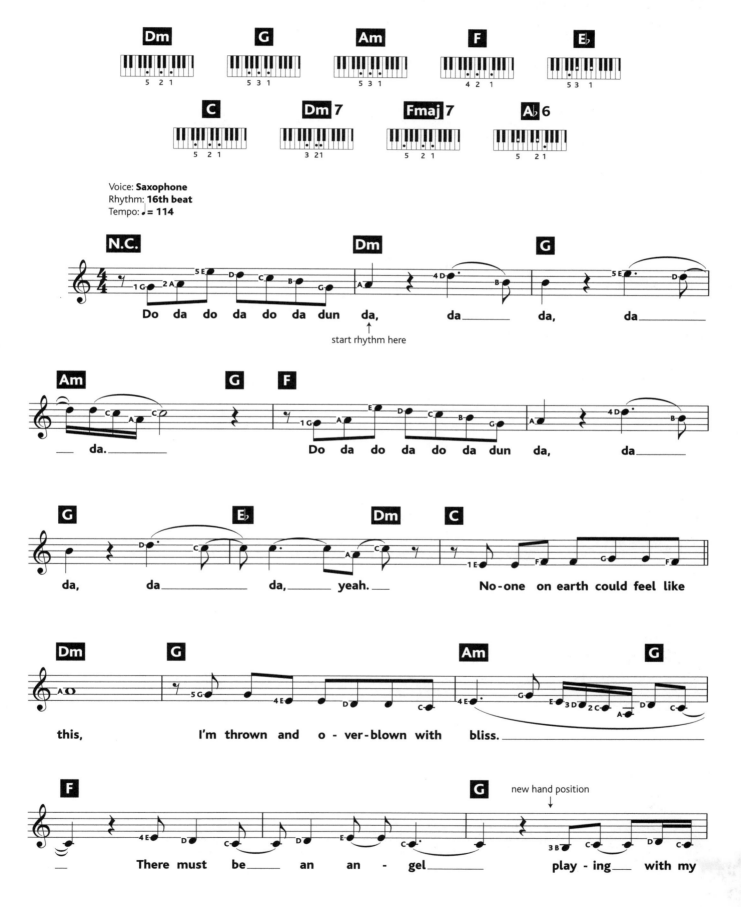

Voice: **Saxophone**
Rhythm: **16th beat**
Tempo: ♩ = 114

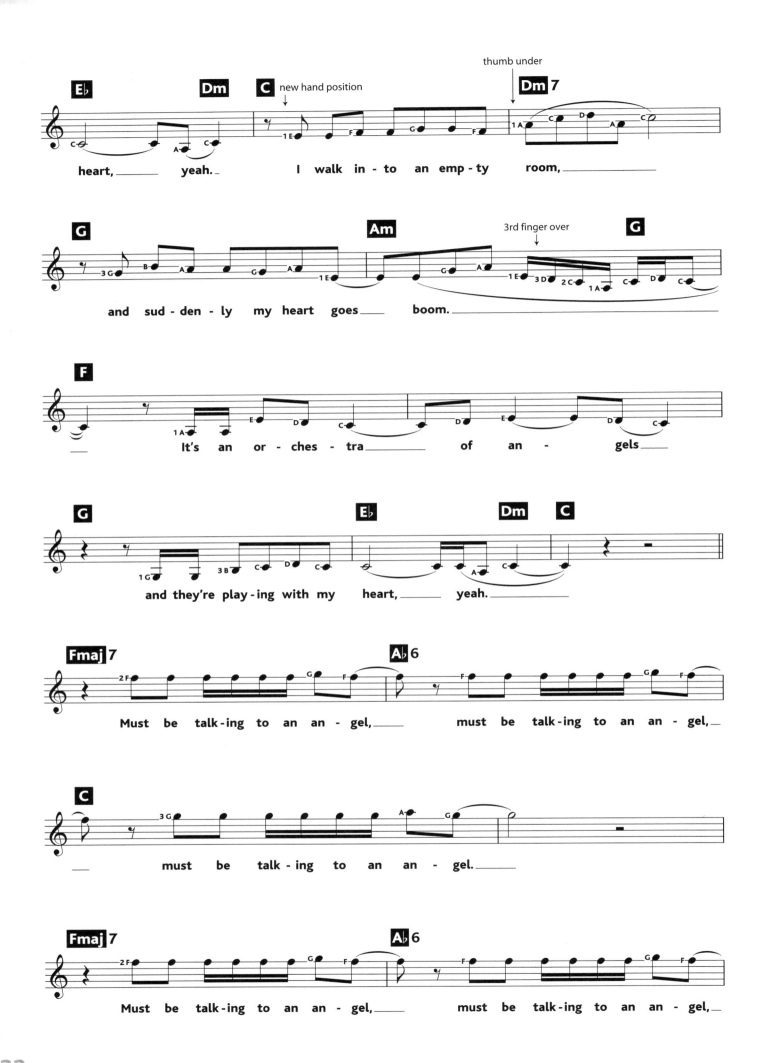

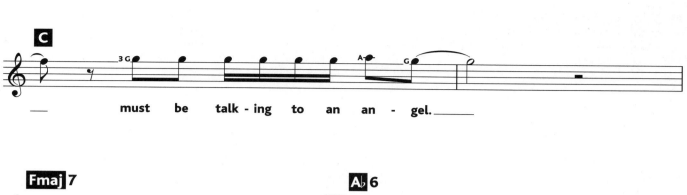

must be talk-ing to an an-gel.

Must be talk-ing to an an-gel,____ must be talk-ing to an an-gel,

must be talk-ing to an an-gel.

Must be talk-ing to an an-gel,____ must be talk-ing to an an-gel,

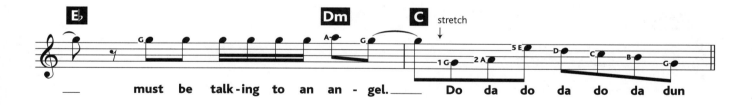

must be talk-ing to an an-gel.____ Do da do da do da dun

da, da____ da, da____ da. Do da do da do da dun

da, da____ da, da____ da,____ yeah.__

2 Become 1

Words & Music by Matt Rowe, Richard Stannard, Melanie Brown, Victoria Adams, Geri Halliwell, Emma Bunton & Melanie Chisholm

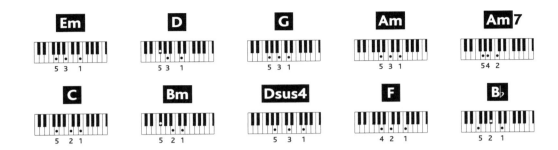

Voice: **Piano**
Rhythm: **Latin**
Tempo: ♩ = **72**

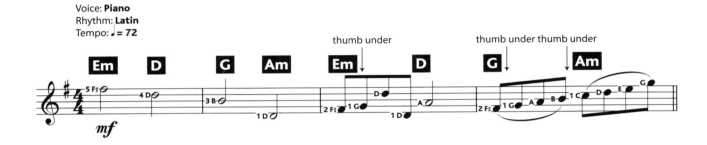

Can - dle light and soul for - ev - er, a dream of you and me to - geth - er.

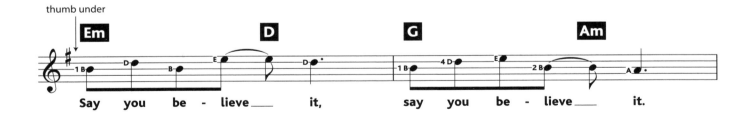

Say you be - lieve ___ it, say you be - lieve ___ it.

Free your mind of doubt and dan - ger, be for real, don't be a strang - er.

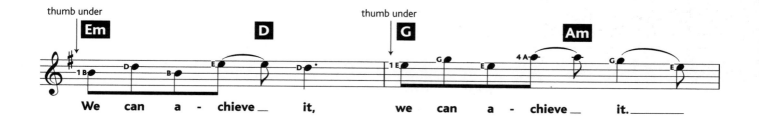

We can a - chieve __ it, we can a - chieve __ it. ____

Come a lit - tle bit clos - er ba - by, ____ get it on, get it on. 'Cause to - night __

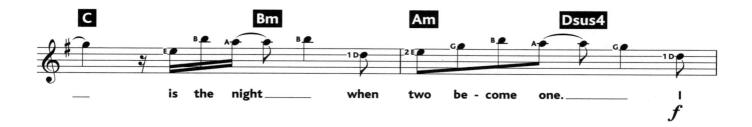

__ is the night ____ when two be - come one. ____ I

need some love like I nev - er need - ed love be - fore, __ (wan - na make love to ya ba - by.) I

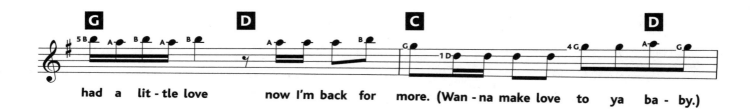

had a lit - tle love now I'm back for more. (Wan - na make love to ya ba - by.)

Set your spir - it free, it's the on - ly way___ to be.___ I

need some love like I nev - er need - ed love be - fore.___ (Wan - na make love to ya ba - by.) I

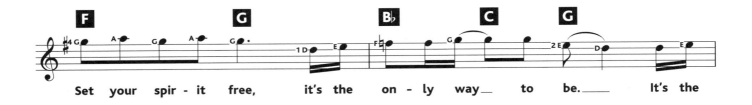

had a lit - tle love now I'm back for more. (Wan - na make love to ya ba - by.)

Set your spir - it free, it's the on - ly way___ to be.___ It's the

on - ly way___ to be.___ It's the on - ly way___ to be.___

stop rhythm here

Umbrella

Words & Music by Christopher Stewart, Terius Nash, Shawn Carter & Thaddis Harrell

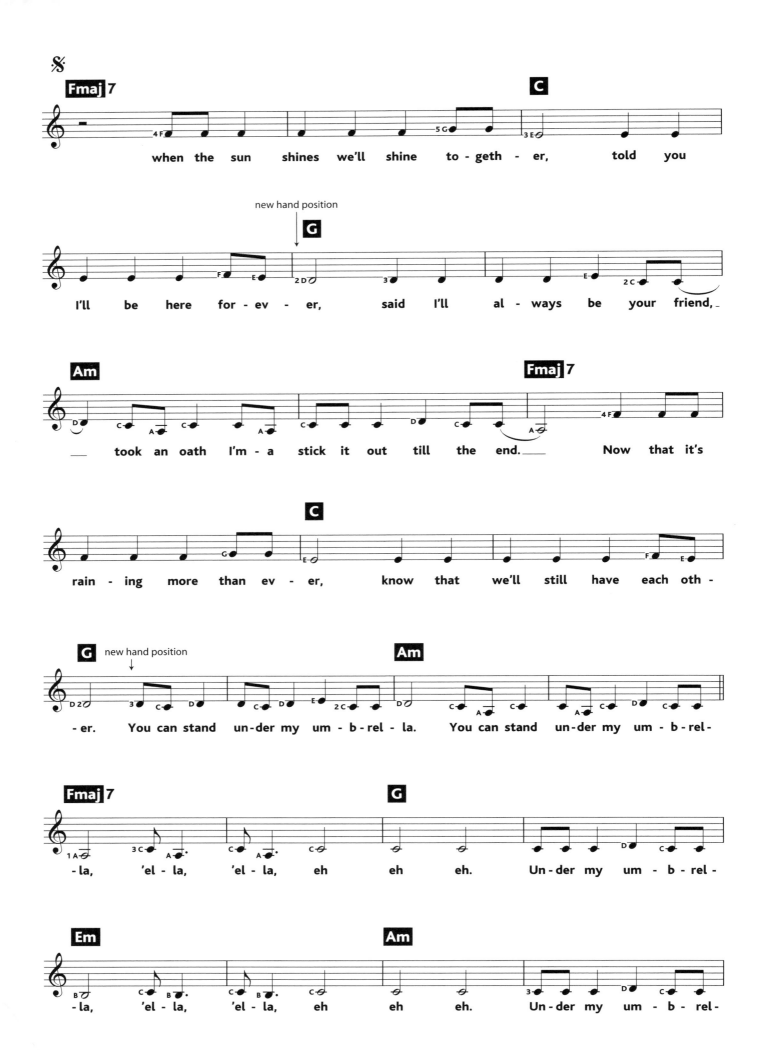

-la, 'el - la, 'el - la, eh eh eh. Un-der my um - b - rel -

-la, 'el - la, 'el - la, eh eh eh eh eh.

You can run____ in - to____ my arms,___ it's o - kay____ don't be___

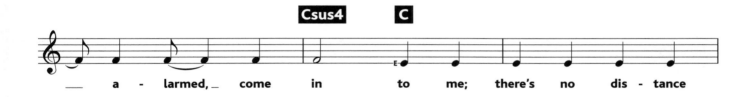

___ a - larmed,__ come in to me; there's no dis - tance

in - bet - ween_____ our love.____ So gon - na

let the rain_____ pour; I'll be all you need and

more._____ Be - cause,

Published by
Wise Publications
14-15 Berners Street, London W1T 3LJ, UK.

Exclusive Distributors:
Music Sales Limited
Distribution Centre, Newmarket Road,
Bury St Edmunds, Suffolk IP33 3YB, UK.
Music Sales Pty Limited
120 Rothschild Avenue, Rosebery, NSW 2018, Australia.

This book © Copyright 2007 Wise Publications,
a division of Music Sales Limited.
Order No. AM992739
ISBN 978-1-84772-455-7

Edited by Sam Harrop.
Music arranged by Paul Honey.
Music processed by Paul Ewers Music Design.
Cover photograph courtesy of LFI.
Printed in the EU.

Your Guarantee of Quality
As publishers, we strive to produce every book
to the highest commercial standards.
This book has been carefully designed to minimise awkward
page turns and to make playing from it a real pleasure.
Particular care has been given to specifying acid-free, neutral-sized paper
made from pulps which have not been elemental chlorine bleached.
This pulp is from farmed sustainable forests and was produced with special
regard for the environment. Throughout, the printing and binding have been
planned to ensure a sturdy, attractive publication which should give years of enjoyment.
If your copy fails to meet our high standards, please inform us and
we will gladly replace it.

www.musicsales.com